Organic jewelry
you can make

LITTLE
CRAFT BOOK
SERIES

BY CARSON I.A. RITCHIE

STERLING
PUBLISHING CO., INC.   NEW YORK
SAUNDERS OF TORONTO, Ltd., Don Mills, Canada

Oak Tree Press Co., Ltd. London & Sydney

Little Craft Book Series

The following photographs were taken by Bernadine Bailey: Illus. 6, 8, 10, 13, 15, 18, 35, 40. S. Mayes Reed took the photographs in Illus. 4, 5, 7, 14, 17, 19, 24, 25, 26, 50, 61. Illus. 33, 53, 62, 64, and 67 were taken by Stella Reid, and Illus. 49 and 51 by Go Gaye. Illus. 3 appears through the courtesy of the Commonwealth Institute, London, England; Illus. 48 through the courtesy of the Allen H. Tinkler Collection, and Illus. 52 through the courtesy of the carvers Hany M. Qumsiyah & Bros., Israel.

Contents

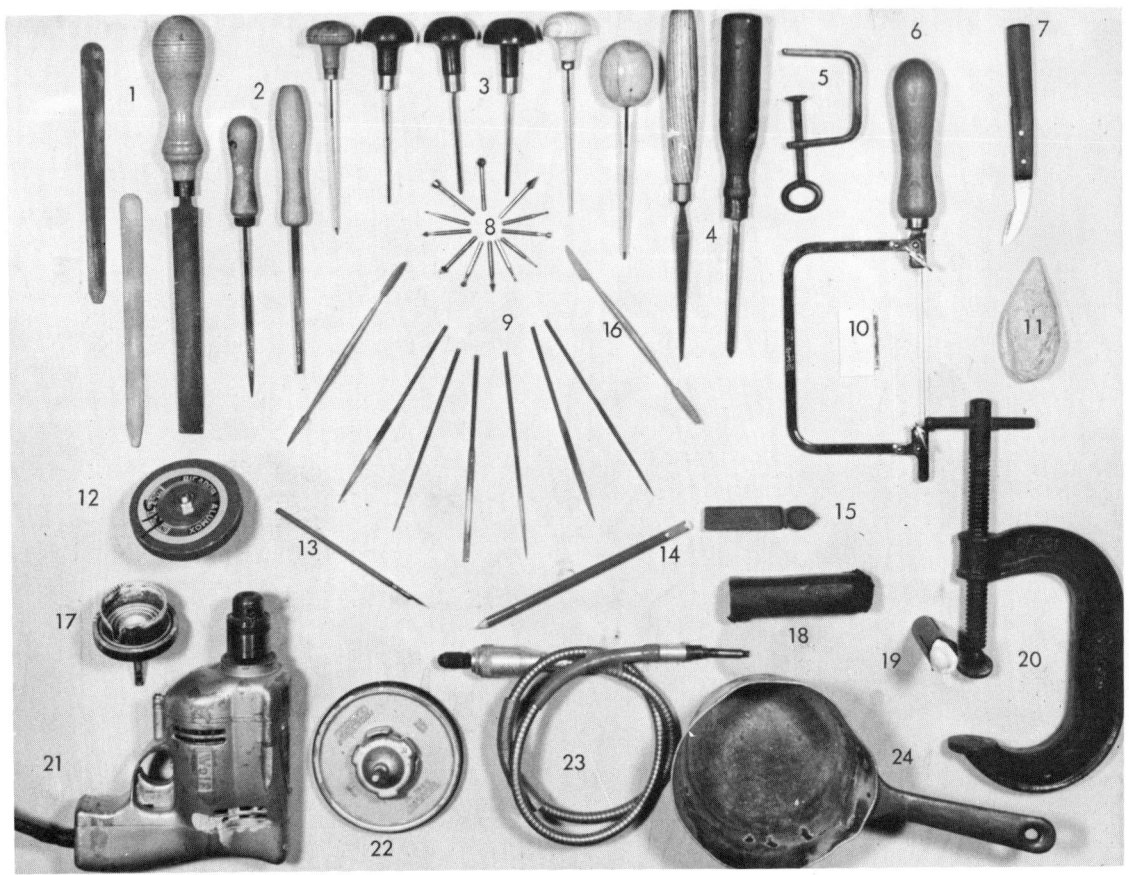

Illus. 1. Tools you will find useful in your organic jewelry-making: **(1)** emery boards; **(2)** files; **(3)** gravers, gouges, veiners; **(4)** wood chisels; **(5)** clamp; **(6)** piercing saw; **(7)** wood engraver's knife; **(8)** rotary files; **(9)** needle files; **(10)** scraper; **(11)** pumice stone block for smoothing and polishing; **(12)** grindstone for electric drill; **(13)** mapping pen for drawing designs with India ink; **(14)** china marker (or grease pencil); **(15)** Eskimo style for engraving scrimshaw; **(16)** riffler; **(17)** rotary saw (hole cutter); **(18)** dop wax; **(19)** dowel for use with dop wax for holding blanks; **(20)** large clamp; **(21)** electric drill; **(22)** sandpaper disc for smoothing down ivory; **(23)** flexible drive to hold rotary files to carve ivory; **(24)** saucepan for boiling tortoise shell and horn.

Before You Begin

Now, as never before, we are living in an age of organic jewelry in which people are buying and wearing adornment ranging from beads of ivory to belts of tortoise shell; from necklaces of seed pods from Haiti to pendants made from the heartwood of African timber trees. Why has this craze for organic jewelry developed?

Many of the materials which were once used for conventional jewelry have now become available in much larger quantities and at lower cost. Naturally, the really rare and precious stones will always remain outside the purchasing power of all but a few. Meanwhile, jewelry-wearers have become tired of the many substitute gems available which are often made up in unattractive materials and badly designed (such as a plastic cameo!) and feel they would rather wear jewelry made from genuine, natural materials—even if they are simple and inexpensive.

Most of the new kind of jewelry, which is made from nuts, beads, and so on, is imported. However, why shouldn't you make the same thing for a tiny percentage of what it costs to buy? Much of the imported jewelry for which people pay highly is made by native craftsmen who are simple folk, without formal training, and who have nothing more than an innate feeling for art and a few simple tools to help them. Some are very young, while others, such as the Italian housewives who make coral beads at Torre del Greco, a suburb of Naples, are quite elderly.

Although organic jewelry is easy to make (after all, Nature has done a lot of the work for you), the materials described in this book stand right in the forefront of art history. Ivory, bone, and horn were the first materials which Man worked into jewelry. Tortoise shell, jet, and coral constituted the next earliest, and were all the subject of very distinguished art work during prehistoric times. All these substances described are still part of the raw material of folk jewelry. Peasant craftsmen all over the world are working in all of them, and this book draws on the many native sources of inspiration which they offer.

There are many reasons why you will enjoy making organic jewelry. You will come in contact with out-of-the-way and romantic substances, as well as lots of ordinary ones to be found in your own back yard, which, perhaps, you have ignored up to now. You will have a chance to find out a little about different cultures and to acquire new skills which will pay off in hobbies other than that of jewelry-making.

The projects are arranged in order of materials, rather than by specific types of jewelry because each material, with its own special characteristics, requires its own way of being treated and turned into jewelry. Every art should work towards some end, as Aristotle remarked, and the end of organic jewelry-making is a product which gives you a real sense of achievement and satisfaction—as well as solving the never-ending problem of Christmas, birthday, and anniversary presents!

Vegetable Materials

Every year Nature lavishes a wealth of raw material for jewelry on us in the shape of fruits, berries, nuts, kernels, and seeds. In many parts of the world great attention is paid to these treasures of the countryside. China produces necklaces made from fruit kernels. Seed pods are woven into attractive necklaces in Haiti. Anyone interested in making organic jewelry will find an abundance of raw material practically on his own door sill.

You can use slack collecting times, such as winter, for either assembling what you collected during the summer, or for working with the imported exotic nuts and seeds described on page 9. Begin collecting by acquiring a pocket-sized, but well illustrated, guide book to trees. Use this guide also to check whether any berries or seeds which you want to collect are poisonous. Avoid all poisonous seed pods, such as those of the laburnum.

A Pine-Cone Pendant

Just to show you how easily you can make a unique piece of organic jewelry, let's make a pendant from a pine cone. Do not choose a large cone, such as one from the maritime pine; instead, select a cone from a tree such as the Atlas cedar, which is shapely, smooth, symmetrical, and only 3 inches long. The Scotch pine has a much more knurled, but attractive, cone of about the right size, and so do the Spanish fir and the Mediterranean cypress. Hemlock and spruce cones make good pendants, as do alder cones.

Illus. 2. Make a pine-cone pendant.

Pick cones before they have opened and dry them thoroughly in a well ventilated cupboard. When a cone is dry, rub it lightly with wax polish or spray with artists' fixative.

Roughen the stem of your cone (Illus. 2) slightly to ensure a good glueing surface before fastening the bell cap onto it. Then attach the cone to the bell cap, using epoxy cement. Squeeze the claws of the cap tightly round the stem and bind with thread to ensure a tight adhesion. When it is completely dry, remove the thread, add a jump ring and pendant chain, and your organic pendant is complete.

6

A Seed-Pod Necklace

There are many seed pods that can be made up into attractive necklaces. Tulip-tree pods and those of the Kentucky coffee tree are good choices. Seed pods are fairly fragile, and although they can be made slightly stronger by spraying them with shellac, you must face the fact that a seed-pod necklace is not going to have a very long life.

You will have the best results if you pick them when they are green, and dry them immediately by immersing in silica gel or in a salt and borax mixture. (This is the method used by the ancient Egyptians for embalming and mummifying.) Then, thoroughly mix powdered laundry borax and dry sand, in the proportion of two-thirds borax to one-third sand. Allow your seed pods to dry thoroughly in this mixture for a week and they will be ready for stringing. You need no jewelry

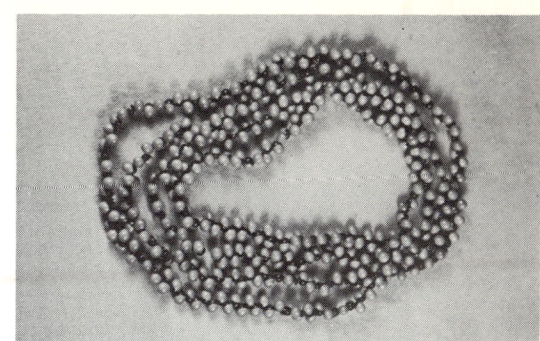

Illus. 3. A necklace of red seeds from Western Samoa.

findings for a seed-pod necklace. Simply make small punctures with a heavy needle, and string the pods on decorative cord or thread which you tie at the nape of the neck.

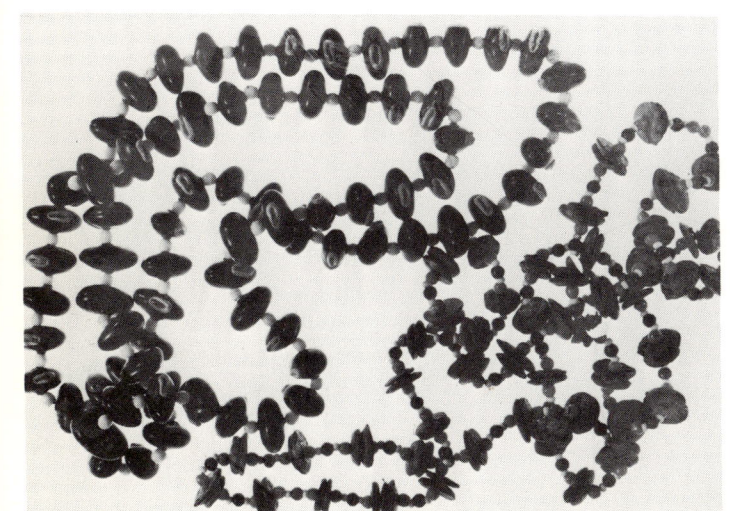

Illus. 4. Bean and seed necklaces from Malawi, Central Africa.

7

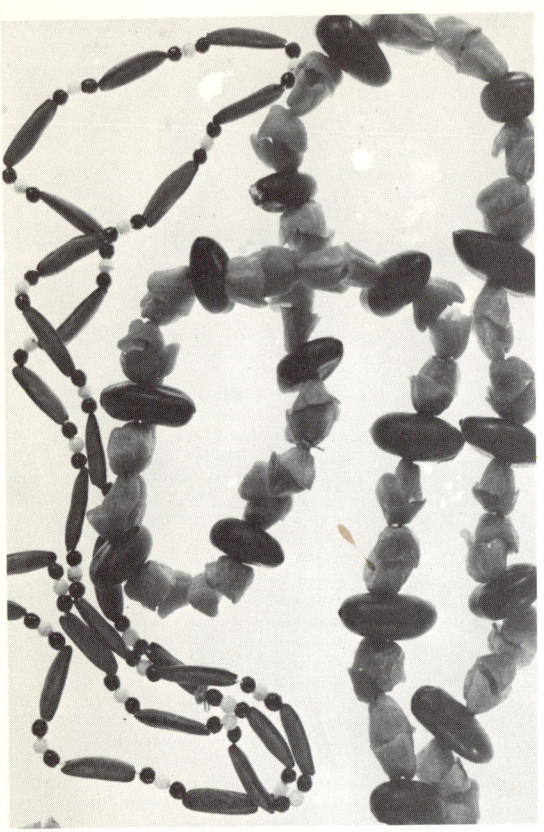

Twirled in a seed, this piercer will make a workable hole just the right size for stringing.

A versatile seed is corn (maize). Use the kernels for husked-corn necklaces and bracelets, or slice the cobs just as you would slice bananas, puncture the middles, and string together for a really exotic-looking necklace. You might also combine the kernels and sliced cobs. Dried peas and beans of various kinds are excellent material for organic jewelry. Try combining different varieties and colors together in one piece of jewelry.

Large fruit stones make ideal brooches and rings. For example, you can make a heart-shaped brooch with a peach stone. If you use a deeply grooved pit, such as the peach, try filling in the crevices with plastic wood which you must then smooth down with sandpaper. You can even make carvings of your own design on fruit stones, or carve them into special shapes. One well known Renaissance lady, the wife of the Bishop of Durham, pleased her dinner guests by carving their portraits right at the table out of the stones of the cherries they had just eaten!

Nineteenth-century craftsmen who made necklaces of fruit stones used to collect olive pits from Italian restaurants, throw them into solution of hot dye, and leave them there for several days. Then they carefully cleaned, scraped, and smoothed them. If the color was not satisfactory, back into the dye they went. Peach pits, hickory nuts, and

Seeds, Nuts, and Berries

Even the most ordinary kinds of seeds make lovely pieces of jewelry. To make a bracelet or necklace from small seeds, you will *not* need a drill. You can pierce them by means of a simple tool you can make yourself. Hammer a long, slender nail into a short length of wood, and then sharpen it on all four sides of the point.

plum pits were given the same treatment, or else simply polished.

Before you use nuts, make sure they are well dried. Bore holes in them for stringing by pushing them through a drill bit held in a flexible drive attached to a power drill (Illus. 6). (Or, if you don't have a flexible drive, put the nut in a vice and use a regular power or hand drill.) Symmetrical nuts such as acorns, hazel nuts, etc., can be strung in line, while asymmetrical ones can be suspended from a line of ordinary beads so that they hang down vertically.

Elaborate rosaries and necklaces were made up during the 19th century from nuts fitted to one another by silver bell caps. If you feel particularly ambitious, this would be a rewarding project, since nuts mounted in silver have an especially fine appearance. Most nuts need no treatment before they are worked on except for the drying process.

Illus. 7. A simple nut pendant.

However, after you drill them, you can polish them lightly with wax polish.

Fruits and berries are, generally speaking, much trickier to handle than seeds and nuts. They are likely to get mouldy and wrinkle up excessively unless you dry them carefully. Use the same drying-out procedure recommended for seed pods. Some berries you can attempt to work with and have a reasonable hope of success are huckleberries, bayberries, green chokeberries, bittersweet, and California pepper fruits.

Inevitably you will want to make jewelry from *exotic* nuts and seeds. Their availability varies a good deal. Occasionally, shell shops and rock shops have some in stock, but you cannot always be sure of getting the kind that you want. On page 47 you will find a list of suppliers of exotic nuts and seeds. To make jewelry from a more "common" exotic nut—the coconut—turn the page.

Illus. 6. Use a drill held in a flexible drive to pierce nuts before stringing.

Coconuts

This aristocrat of exotic nuts has been very neglected by jewelry-makers, although some fine craftwork has been done with it, especially in Ceylon, where elaborate tea sets of coconut and ivory are made.

The coconut has a thick fibrous husk, enclosing the nut itself. The nut has a woody shell, and this is what you will work on. Begin by removing the shell from the husk and smoothing off any clinging fibrous material. (The fibre is what is used in making mats, etc.) You will notice three "eyes" at the top of the shell. The largest one is very easily punctured. Pour out the milk (and drink it if you like it), and then either saw the shell in two with a cabinet saw, or simply break it in two with a hammer and chisel. Then scoop out the meat.

Clamp the rim of the shell in a vice. Take a hole-cutter from which the central drill has been sawed away, fit it into an electric drill, and cut away a number of roundels from the shell (Illus. 8). Use these for brooches, bracelets, or pendants.

You can also cut out half-moons and ellipses with the hole-cutter by superimposing one cut on top of another (Illus. 9). Double-axe shapes can also be made with the hole-cutter. Half-moons, or crescents, are excellent for earrings and cuff links. String together ellipses for necklaces or bracelets, or use as ring stones and earrings. Double-axe shapes make attractive cuff links and ring stones.

Every part of a coconut shell is slightly rounded, though you can file really small pieces almost flat. Usually, you will use the convex side for the face of your piece of jewelry. Because it is curved, however, coconut shell will crack easily if you screw it up in a vice carelessly. Grip the piece you are working on in a hand vice, clamp it in a leather-lined vice, or wrap it in a piece of cloth and clamp it in an ordinary vice. You can also work on a piece by sticking it down on your work surface with a blob of melted beeswax.

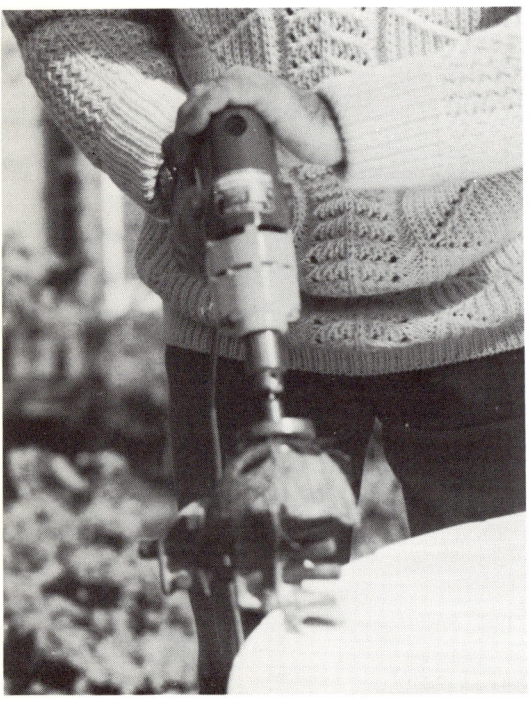

Illus. 8. Use a hole-cutter held in an electric drill to cut as many discs as you want from a coconut shell half which is held in a vice.

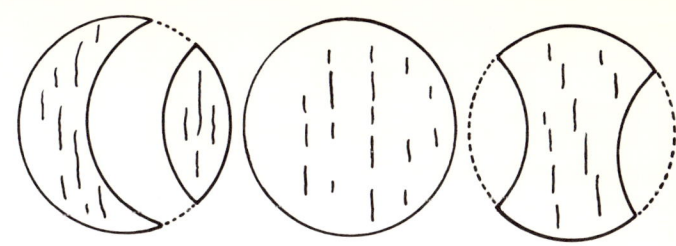

Illus. 9. You can easily cut jewelry blanks of different shapes from coconut shell by superimposing one cut made by the hole-cutter upon another.

The outside surface of the coconut is a dark brown marked with thin yellow streaks here and there. You will find these streaks are softer than the surrounding shell and tend to go into the surface fairly deeply. For this reason, avoid using a piece of shell that has too many of these streaks.

Smooth down the surface of the shell with a medium file, being careful to file out all the yellow streaks, if possible. Then smooth with sandpaper—first, with coarse, then with medium, and finally with fine.

After you have completed the fine-sandpaper rubbing, you should have a nicely polished piece of shell, because the oil in the coconut acts as a natural polishing medium. If you are not satisfied, however, polish with wax furniture polish or French polish (shellac dissolved in denatured alcohol). If you use the French polish, rub down between coats with fine sandpaper, and give a final polish with a soft cloth (Illus. 10). Another

Illus. 10. Applying French polish (shellac and denatured alcohol) to a coconut brooch to polish it.

11

Illus. 12. Design for a circular carved brooch which you can carry out in coconut, tortoise shell, ivory, or wood.

idea is to paint the coconut with polyurethane varnish. If, for some reason, you wish to darken the shell (although it is naturally fairly dark), rub it with linseed oil.

The most effective ornamentation for coconut is a fretwork design (Illus. 11). Trace a fretwork pattern, using a graver, onto a jewelry blank, such as one of the roundels which you cut with the hole-cutter. Outline the design in Chinese white ink, using a mapping pen (Illus. 1). With a fine drill, drill holes through all the sections to be cut out. Then place the blank on a sawing pin and cut out all the portions of the design to be removed. Fretwork is not easy, so do not attempt it until you have gained considerable experience.

Inlaying

If you wish, you can use your pierced design for making inlays. Ivory and coconut combine well together. Make up some square or triangular

Illus. 11. Fretwork consists of straight lines and bars arranged in symmetrical patterns. These four examples are of Greek origin.

12

rods of ivory (see page 22), together with some round rods which are the exact size of a twist drill bit. Make drill holes in the shell where you want round ivory spots. Many ivory offcuts have a square or triangular section just right for inlaying. You can easily round them off with a file for round inlays.

Where you want to insert a square or triangular piece, lay the end of a rod of ivory against the coconut and use it as a template. Draw round it with the point of a style (Illus. 1). Cut out the shape with a piercing saw.

Then, dip the end of one of the rods in wood glue and push it into a hole which fits it. Saw it off flush with the surface of the coconut, using a piercing saw. Go on to filling in all of the other holes in the same way.

You might also inlay coconut shell with thin silver strips. Cut lines in the surface of the shell and force glue-smeared strips into them.

Illus. 13. Carve coconut with a graver (see Illus. 1), using a piece of thick carpeting as a support.

Bone and Horn

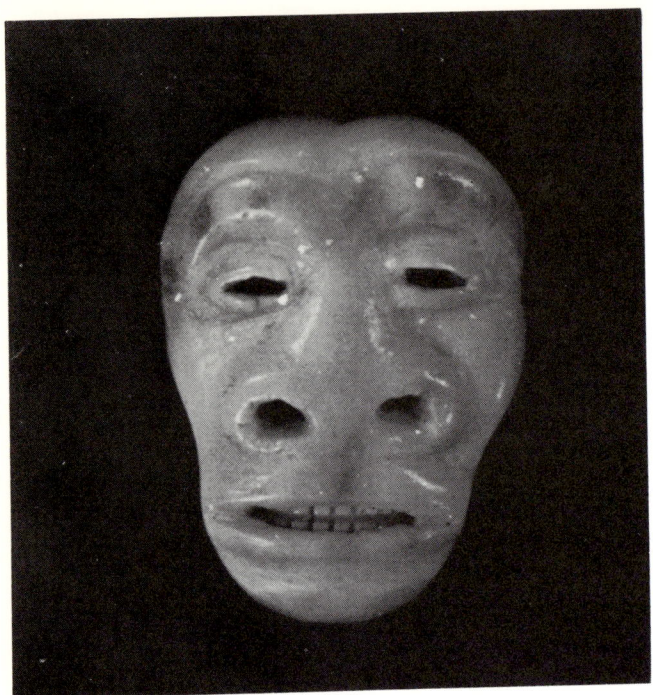

Illus. 14. A staghorn mask with ivory teeth and black glass eyes could also be mounted on a brooch or used as a pendant.

You should have no trouble obtaining bones from a butcher or slaughter-house. Although the shin-bones of horses and cattle are ideal for carving, you should have no great difficulty with the bones from more common cuts of beef. Ready-made bone blanks of various sizes are available at hobby shops and craft supply houses. Another good source of high quality bone is a bone folder which you can usually find in an art supply or stationery shop. An average-sized bone folder will yield enough material for a pair of earrings, several cuff links, and a pendant or two. Old household knives with bone handles are well worth salvaging

—generally, the bone used was the best quality available and can be bleached and used again.

To bleach bone, steep it in a solution of household bleach. Avoid hydrogen peroxide, which works well but is likely to burn your fingers if it splashes on them. In any case, use rubber gloves and take care the bleach does not splash in your eyes. Regulate the amount of bleach to the degree of color in the bone. Too strong a solution will reduce the bone to a chalky white, while too little will have no effect. Experiment and observe the results carefully.

Bones from the kitchen or butcher need a

thorough cleaning. To remove the fatty matter and oil from bones, first boil and dry them. Then suspend them on heavy thread or cord in a glass jar containing turpentine. Place the jar in sunlight for a minimum of 30 hours. By that time, a heavy liquid should have settled in the bottom of the jar. Decant the clear turpentine on top and use again. Throw the sediment away.

Carve bone with saws, files, gravers, burins, and sculptors' rifflers (Illus. 1). Carve flat pieces by fixing them down on your worktable with lapidary cement (16 parts pitch, 2 parts resin, 4 parts shellac, and 1 part beeswax). This is available from craft houses and is called "dop wax." Bones are

not very thick and jewelry you make from them must therefore be flat or round. Because the middle of any bone is spongy and unusable, carve only the outside part.

To polish carved bone, brush in a thick creamy paste of whiting and water and then brush it off with cold water. Give it a final polish with a stiff brush. Other polishing compounds you might try are: fine brick dust and water or charcoal and water, followed by whiting or precipitated chalk; fine tripoli powder (rotten stone) or fine pumice powder, followed by putty powder.

Unlike bone, horn can be boiled, and then pressed flat or bent into shape. Actually, horn has

Illus. 15. Use a hacksaw to cut a horn into blanks for rings, brooches, and such. See Illus. 16 for stages in making a ring.

15

Illus 16. Four stages in making a horn ring. Cut a blank (1). Mark the circle to be cut out with a china marker. Drill two holes to admit a piercing-saw blade (2). Cut the circle out (3). File and sandpaper to shape, then polish (4).

characteristics similar to tortoise shell (below). Place it in boiling water and leave it until it is really soft. You will find you can cut it up, or twist it into whatever shape you wish. While the horn is soft, you can easily punch out roundels to use for brooches, cuff links, or rings (Illus. 16).

Tortoise Shell

The best tortoise shell is the horny mottled plate material covering the carapace (top) of the tropical hawksbill turtle, the smallest of the sea turtles and not an endangered species. (Other tortoise shell tends to be opaque, soft and leathery.) The mottled plates are very thin, and

though the shell consists of horny matter, it is much harder and more brittle than horn.

Tortoise shell is used in large quantities by eyeglass frame-makers. These craftsmen select the best parts of the shell, and the left-over pieces can be acquired at low cost.

Another kind of tortoise shell which is also very inexpensive is "scabby shell," which are plates that have either split a little or have been marked by a limpet who settled on the turtle's back. Unusable by the professional, they are ideal for your purposes. Avoid the "blonde," or yellow, shell which comes from the underbelly (plastron) of the turtle. It is more expensive than the dark kind, but does not show up as well in jewelry pieces. (See page 47 for suppliers.)

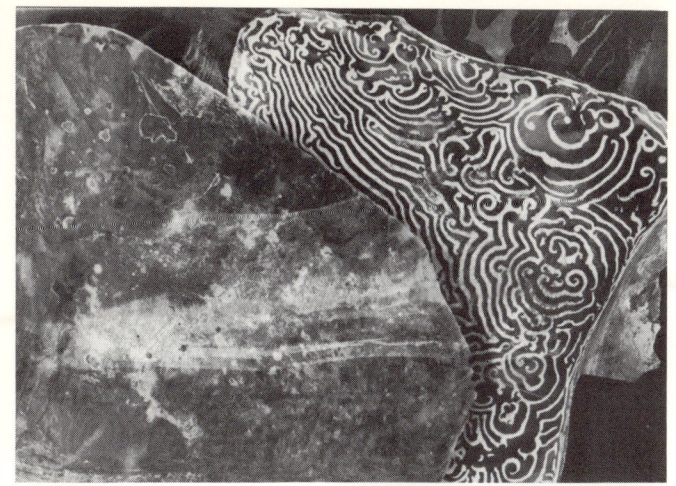

Illus. 17. Natural plates of tortoise shell. On the left is the underside, and on the right the top.

Illus. 18. Hold the plate on a sawing pin while you saw with a piercing saw. A sawing pin is a narrow board which has a V-cut in the end, inside which the blade of the saw operates.

Cuff Links and Earrings

You will find readily available lozenge-shaped pieces of tortoise shell, left by the eyeglass frame-maker, which he cut out for the lenses to be inserted. Select two of these pieces for your cuff links. Since these usually have a drill hole on one end made before the inside of the frames were cut, you will have to saw that end off with a piercing saw. Then smooth off the edges with a file, followed by progressively finer grades of sandpaper. Be very careful not to scratch the surface.

When they are smooth as possible, dip a cloth in almond or olive oil spread with tripoli powder, and polish the pieces. Be sure to polish both sides because tortoise shell is translucent. Then take a fresh cloth, dip in oil as before, spread with plate powder (used for polishing silver plate), and polish the shell until it has a high gloss. Rub with a third cloth dipped in oil only, and finish with a dry cloth. Do not be satisfied until you can see the reflection of your face in the shell. Then attach cuff link or earring findings with epoxy cement.

Bracelets and Necklaces

Select a group of lozenges (you can purchase them by the pound) more or less the same size. In order to make them exactly the same size, make a pattern, and mark each with a grease pencil, a china marker or a mapping pen dipped in Chinese white. Then saw them to size with a piercing saw. Shape and polish as for the cuff links and earrings.

Arrange the lozenges in a straight line between two parallel straightedges, or rulers, to keep them from shifting. With the china marker, draw a line through the middle of each as a guide for drilling a hole on each end of the lozenges with a fine twist drill bit. Thread a piece of elastic through the holes and tie a knot on the end.

Illus. 19. Tortoise shell offcuts left by the eyeglass frame-maker include lozenges and edge cuts. Note the characteristic drill holes in the lozenges.

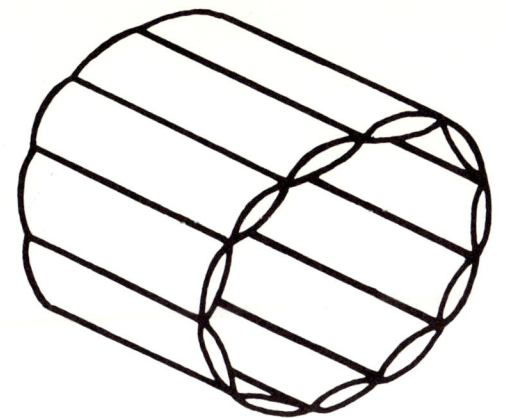

Illus. 20. Here is a bracelet you can make from the tortoise-shell lozenges left by the eyeglass frame-maker.

Rings

You can make a ring in the same way as you did the cuff links or earrings. However, when you mount the polished shell on the finding, attach a piece of silver or gold foil to the underside of it with wood cement. This will cause a light reflection which is very attractive. Then cut a thin piece of tortoise shell which is not good enough to use where it will show, and attach it to the bottom of the foil. This will prevent the foil from wearing off.

Tortoise shell has an unusual characteristic: it can be heated in boiling water until it softens. This quality makes it possible for you to mould it, twist it, or build it up in layers.

To make another kind of ring, cut out a roundel about *half the size* you want your ring to be. Drill a hole in the middle of it with a piercing saw. Then boil the roundel for at least an hour in water to which a quarter-cup of salt for every pint of water has been added. (Tortoise shell varies in the time it takes to get really soft, so you might experiment on a scrap piece first.)

Test the roundel for softness by removing it from the water with a spoon and trying to bend it between your fingers (wear gloves so you won't be burned). If you feel it is pliable enough, slip it on a wooden dowel the exact size of the finished ring. If this is difficult to do, return the shell to the boiling water. Keep testing until it slips on the dowel easily. Tortoise shell dries and hardens quite quickly when it is removed from heat. Leave the ring on the dowel overnight, and it will have set completely in its new shape by morning.

Then round off any roughness on the ring with a file and a craft knife. Smooth with sandpaper, and polish as described on page 18.

 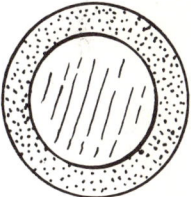

Illus. 21. Eyeglass frames are cut small and then forced apart under pressure after the shell has been boiled and softened. In the same way, you can make a small thick ring into a larger one by using a dowel or split peg and wedge.

19

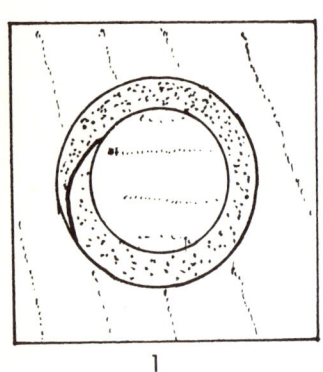
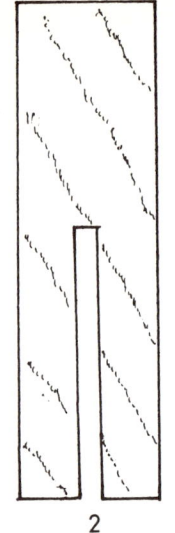

Illus. 22. Clamp for welding rings: (1) wood clamp with hole in middle in which strip of tortoise shell is fitted; (2) split peg which is driven into the middle of ring; (3) wedge which is driven into split peg.

Welding

Welding consists of joining one or more pieces of tortoise shell together. Take two pieces of shell exactly the same size. Roughen one surface of each slightly by rubbing it on coarse sandpaper. Boil the two pieces until soft. Fit them together precisely, rough side to rough side, and place them in a wood clamp. Screw it tightly and return to the boiling water for a short time. Remove and allow to cool before unclamping.

Rings, as well as flat pieces, can also be made from welded tortoise shell. Cut a straight piece of shell the width of the ring you want to make, and just long enough so that the two ends will overlap slightly when the ring is formed. Roughen and slightly taper the two ends. Boil the strip until soft.

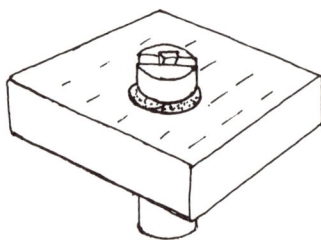

Illus. 23. Assembled clamp, ready to be dropped into boiling water. Wood will expand and tortoise-shell ends will be bonded together.

Remove and twist it round a wooden dowel the exact size of the inside measurement of the ring. Overlap the two ends and tape them tightly together. Return to the boiling water for a short time. Remove and cool. You can make bangle earrings or a bracelet the same way.

20

Inlaying

You can easily force pieces of inlay into softened shell. Use either thin sheet silver, available from craft houses, or an old silver coin, if you have one. File the piece to be inlayed until it is smooth and then polish it with sandpaper.

Boil the tortoise shell to be inlayed. When soft, remove, and set the inlay on it quickly. Sandwich the shell and inlay between two small pieces of wood and compress the whole thing in a wood clamp. Leave overnight to set. You will find the inlay is permanently set into the shell.

Carving

Tortoise shell is easily carved. Use the same tools that you use for carving ivory—gravers, gougers, burins, and cutting knives (see page 4). Although it has a somewhat "tacky" resistance to the graver, you only need a little experience to achieve just the right touch. To overcome the resistance of the shell, rock the point of the tool a little as you work.

Polish your finished carvings by rubbing with pieces of sandpaper or brushing them with wet, powdered pumicestone.

Illus. 24. The cuff links on the right have a silver inlay in the form of the letter "S". The cuff links on the left are made with snail's opercula (page 29) and the ring at the top is made with jet (page 44).

21

Ivory

Ivory is surprisingly inexpensive—at least the kind that we recommend. In the past, and still too often, animals have been threatened with extinction because of indiscriminate slaughter far beyond the needs of civilization. This is most particularly true of elephants and other animals who are not prolific breeders. Since ivory is used for very specific purposes, scraps are always available of the less desirable parts, and rather than let them go to

waste completely, you can use them to good advantage in your jewelry-making.

Such scraps are offcuts from the main tusk—the tip or the hollow end. Other scraps include the odd cuts left by craftsmen who make piano keys. These offcuts are usually triangular in shape and you can saw them up into triangular beads or cuff links. Soft elephant ivory is the best, and while it is the most expensive, you need very little of it to make jewelry. Because only the best ivory is used for piano-key veneers, these offcuts are completely white and do not have any of the cream-colored streaks sometimes found on other ivories.

Bark slips are also left by the piano-key cutter. These are the original husks of the outside of the tusk and are often smokey brown or have a black-etched pattern of fine interlacing cracks. These are ideal for making jewelry which does not require

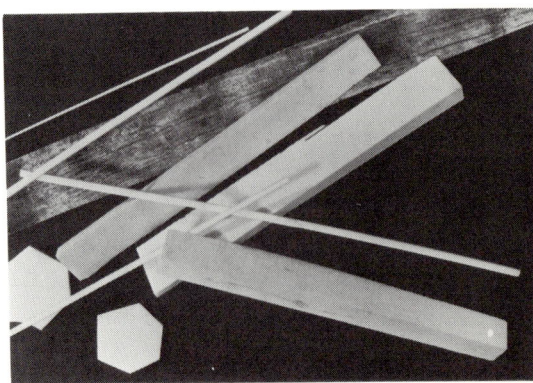

Illus. 26. Offcuts left by the piano-key veneer-maker are ideal raw material for jewelry. They include triangles, rods, bark slips, and octagons.

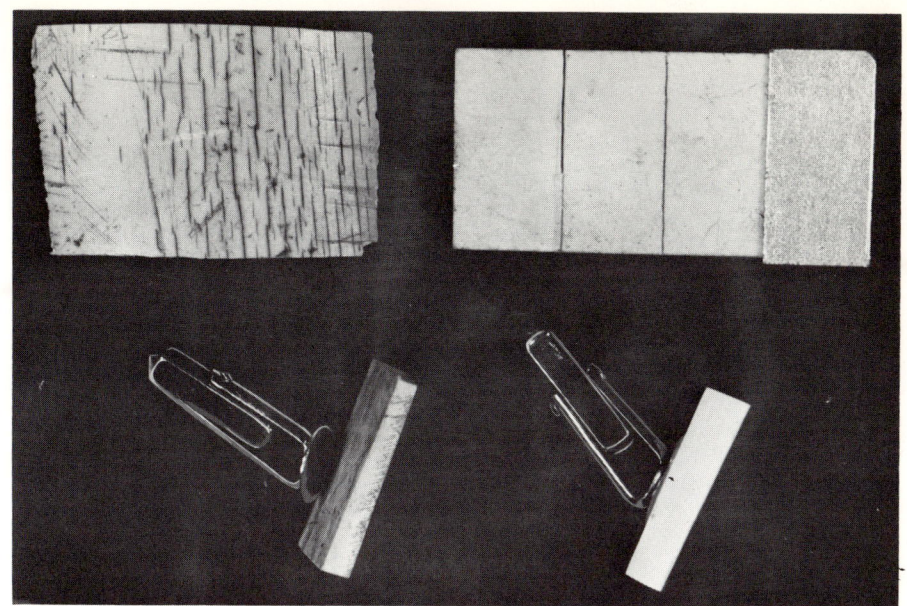

Illus. 27. Stages in making cuff links from bark slips of ivory. The bark slip is shown at top left. At top right a metal template the size of the desired cuff link was used to mark it out, and then the pieces into shape with a jeweler's saw. After polishing, the links are attached to the findings (below).

any shaping or polishing. Simply cut out the outline of the piece of jewelry with a piercing saw and leave the surface plain to show off its exotic color and pattern. You can obtain both kinds of offcuts from the ivory suppliers listed on page 47. Specify that you want bark slips and triangular offcuts left from piano-key veneers and order about a pound of each mixed together.

Other kinds of offcuts can be bought from any ivory warehouse. They include the hollow tusk ends, which are ideal for making bangles or bracelets. The farther the tusk end is from the part of the tusk which fits into the mouth, the more expensive the ivory, because there is a smaller cavity and a larger amount of good ivory. Try to estimate what size bangle you want to make and ask the ivory warehouse to select a tusk end which will meet your requirements.

You can obtain very useful scrap from warehouses in the form of old billiard balls, or pieces of carved ivory that have been broken. Any kind of scrap will make some kind of jewelry.

Then, there are the lesser-known kinds of ivory: hippopotamus teeth, wart-hog tusks, and whale's teeth. Hippo teeth are inexpensive, but they have a hard porcellaneous enamel on the outside curve of

23

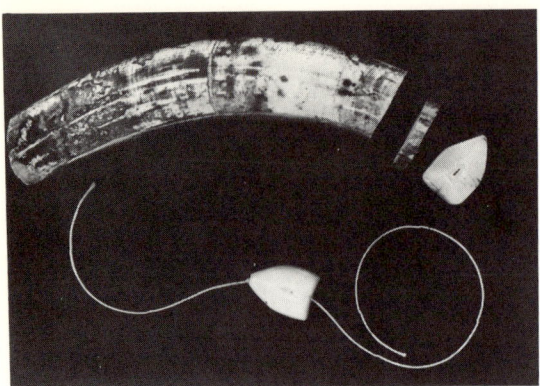

Illus. 28. A boar's tusk provides instant beads or pendants. Just saw across it using a hacksaw. Shape and polish the cut-off piece with a file. Polish and drill it for a thread.

the tooth which must be stripped off with a grindstone. Buy only the large teeth because the smaller are liable to have cracks and yellow lines in them.

Wart-hog tusks and boar's tusks are useful because they can be sawed across at right angles and turned into irregularly shaped beads. Like whale's teeth, boar's tusks show a marked color variation, the outside of the tusk being darker than the inside. Very attractive whale's tooth jewelry is made in Iceland by the simple method of sawing across a tooth, and from the section, making an oval (cabochon) brooch. The middle of the whale's tooth is *café au lait* and shows up in marked contrast to the outside, which is milky white in color.

Once you have acquired a stock of ivory, store it somewhere fairly cold. If it is kept in a warm temperature, it may split.

Cut your ivory into the sizes you want with an ordinary saw or hacksaw. Clamp the ivory down onto the edge of your workbench or hold it in a vice. Start the cut with a triangular-shaped file. Lubricate the cut well with water poured on with a sprinkler of some kind.

The most useful tool for working ivory is the file. Keep a stock of these, especially needle files (Illus. 1). For carving, use gravers, burins, and chisels. Although a hand vice is useful for holding pieces while you are filing, you can make a simple tool yourself for that purpose. Cut a wooden dowel (or even a broom handle) to a length convenient to grasp. Drill a hole in the middle and insert a needle with the point broken off. Use this for holding the piece of scrap ivory which you are now going to make into beads.

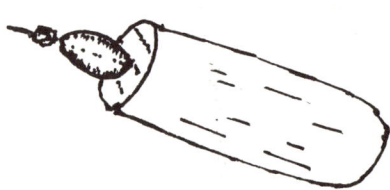

Illus. 29. A home-made bead holder.

Ivory Beads

Making beads from ivory is easy. Saw up some ivory scraps, such as the hollow end of a tusk, into cubes or oblongs (Illus. 28). Put each one into a vice and drill through it with a fine twist drill bit. Slip a bead blank over the shank of the broken needle of your home-made tool. Cement it to the wooden handle with dop wax (page 4). Then with a file, shape the bead into the form you have

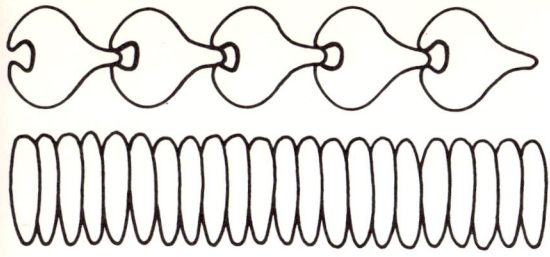

Illus. 30. These two necklaces, made by the Erbach Craft School in Germany, could easily be cut from bark slips.

Buttons

Make a set of fancy buttons from bark slips for a special suit or dress. Cut out a cardboard template for the buttons. If your buttons are to be round, use a compass to get a perfect circle. Lay the pattern on the cut side of the slip and trace it on with a sharp pencil. Saw round the pencil outline with a piercing saw, round off the rough edges with a file, and smooth them with a piece of fine sandpaper. Stick on a button shank (available from hobby shops) with epoxy cement, and go on to your next button.

chosen. (Suggestions for designs for bead shapes are shown in Illus. 30.)

When all your beads are formed, string them on a wire, tie it to a board, and you can polish them all together easily. Begin by rubbing with a file; then smoothing with medium sandpaper, followed by fine sandpaper. Finish with the finest sandpaper, "flour paper," and then rub with damp pumice powder on a brush. Follow this by a brushing with damp putty powder (oxide of tin) or finely powdered whiting. Finish by rubbing with a dry cotton cloth, rolled into a sausage.

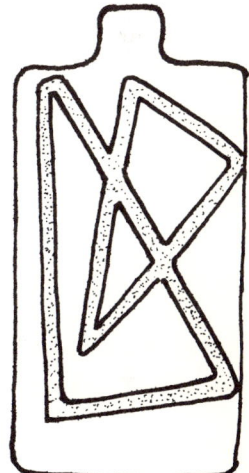

Illus. 32. Pendant design by Albert G. Theodor Mayer.

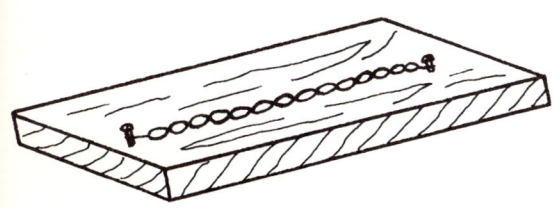

Illus. 31. String beads onto a wire held by two screws on a board for "mass-production" polishing.

Pendants

To make a simple pendant, draw an interesting shape on a bark slip, allowing for a hole at the top of the pendant for a thong or chain. Cut out the design with the piercing saw. Illus. 32 shows how striking a simple design in ivory can be. Or, make

Illus. 33. Ivory brooches carved by Marko Scott of Malawi. He files, sandpapers, then polishes them with metal polish.

a more elaborate pendant by cutting a thin slab of ivory, drawing your chosen shape on it, and cutting it out with the piercing saw as before. Then, ornament it with a carved design (Illus. 33), or cut out hollows which you can inset with semi-precious stones such as amber, turquoise, or jet. Polish as described for beads.

You can make very sophisticated pendants in several ways. If you have an old billiard ball made of ivory (modern balls are not), saw out the middle portion of it, sandpaper it smooth, and then scratch on a design with a sharp nail set in a wooden peg. (You can also use a graver.) When you finish the design, fill it in with black India ink, using a mapping pen. The lines will stand up in a beautiful black relief against the white background (Illus. 34). This technique is called "scrimshaw."

For a really elegant pendant, try making a fretwork design. Cut a thin slice of ivory, and draw on it a fretwork pattern (Illus. 11). Drill through the spaces to be cut out by inserting the blade of a piercing saw in each space (Illus. 35). Cut, and then smooth the insides of the cuts with a needle file. Hold a piece of fine sandpaper on your workbench and rub the face of the pendant on it to finish it off. Ivory will not break when you are doing fretwork, as coconut shell does, but practice first with the coconut until you have conquered

26

the technique (see page 12). Mother-of-pearl shell also can be your practice material as it is less expensive than ivory, although more brittle.

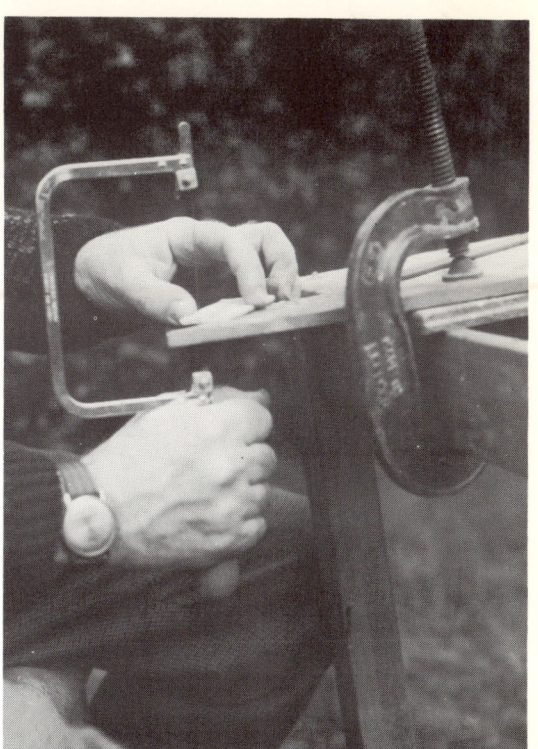

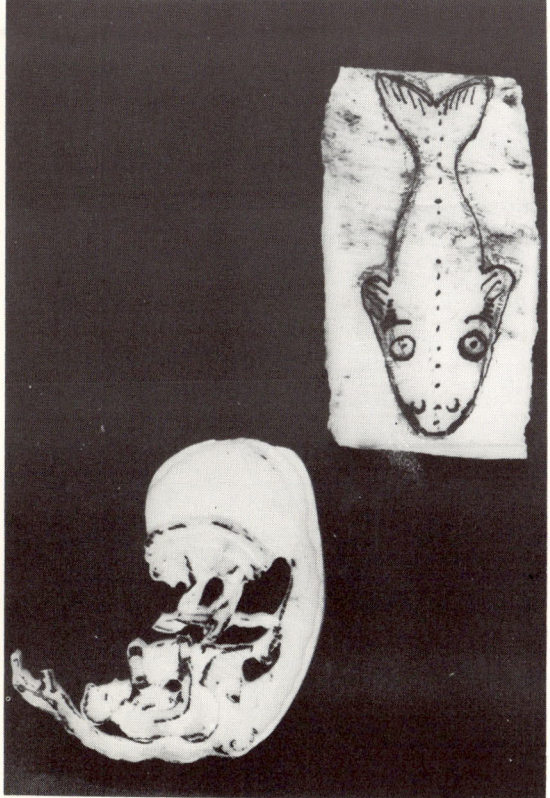

Illus. 34. The fish brooch on the right is outlined with India ink, while the shape on the left has been sawed out with a jeweler's saw.

Bangles, Bracelets, and Rings

Bangles or bracelets are easily cut from hollow tusk ends. Often you will find a tusk end with a split or crack, and if you must use it, fill in the crack with epoxy cement mixed with a little ivory dust. Allow to set and you will be able to cut through it easily. Sand and polish your finished pieces as before.

Other odd scraps of cut ivory are useful for these small pieces of jewelry. Buy metal blanks

27

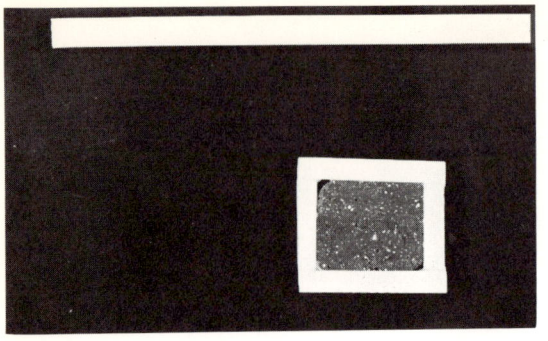

Illus. 36. Brooches, earrings, cuff links, or rings can easily be made from ivory offcuts such as shown here at the top. Cut the rod into four short pieces and cement them together. Use colored sealing wax to fill the space in the middle so that it is on a level with the ivory rods. File and polish with sandpaper. Small ivory fragments could be set in the wax in "mosaic" fashion also.

which are made for enamelled jewelry and have a rim round them. Mix some colored sealing wax (black, red, or blue are the most effective) with denatured alcohol. Arrange some small ivory fragments into a pattern within the rims of the blank. Spread the wax with a palette knife into the area between the fragments, until it is on a level with them (Illus. 36). Rub down with a file and polish with fine sandpaper and polishing powders.

One of the most unusual pieces of jewelry you can make is an ivory signet ring. Measure the finger first. Then cut out a round blank using a piercing saw. Outline the circumference of the finger on the blank, and then make a drill hole in the middle. Insert the piercing saw blade, and saw round. File smooth. Carve out a bezel with a graver and then carve your monogram. You might apply this same technique to a pair of cuff links or a tie tack.

Illus. 37. Two ivory blanks. The one on the left has been pierced with a drill, and a plug of a dark-colored wood inserted and glued into the hole. The one on the right is in the process of being carved into a starfish tie tack.

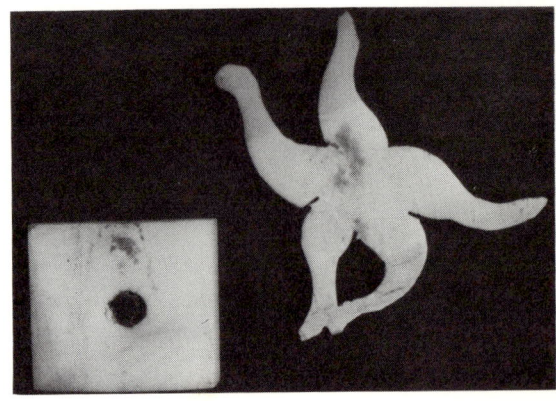

Shells

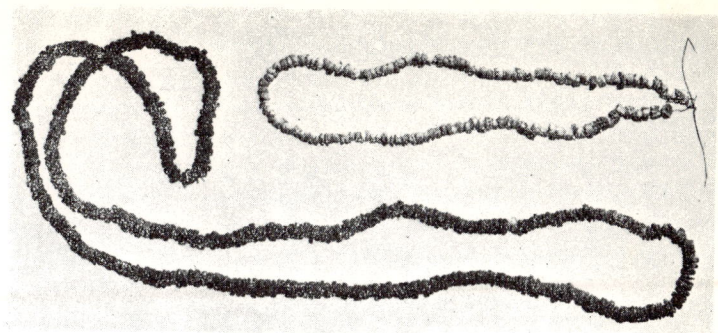

Illus. 38. These old strings of shell-bead money are from the Solomon Islands. Such shell necklaces, armlets, and bracelets are more highly valued than any other form of currency.

There are so many wonderful shells to use for making jewelry, including the ordinary little shells you find at the seashore, that the first thing to do is acquire an identification guide to shells. You can find most shells available in shell shops or, better yet, in shell warehouses, which you can assemble right away into pieces of jewelry.

From a shell warehouse you can order a whole bagful of small shells to use as beads for necklaces and bracelets—for the price of one ready-made shell necklace! You can buy already-polished iridescent shells from a shell shop and attach them to a pendant chain with a little epoxy cement. One of the least expensive and most attractive shells available in shell shops is the operculum of the snail (Illus. 39). This tiny "front door" with

Illus. 39. You can easily attach a snail's operculum onto a finding.

which some snails are equipped can be immediately fitted onto earring, cuff-link or tie-tack findings.

One thing your shell guide will *not* tell you is which shells are the most difficult to work on and which are the easiest. Shells vary a great deal in hardness according to their chemical composition. Scratching shells with a file will soon tell you which are harder. Some shells are difficult to work with because they have awkward shapes, for example, razor shells and some scallops, while still others have spiny parts that might catch on clothing. Avoid difficult shells of any kind for your first shell project.

Coral

The easiest shell material to begin work on is coral, which grows on the sea bottom at depths below five fathoms in the form of tiny trees or bushes. Precious red coral grows well below the surface, is hard, compact, has a lively color, and is so small it could never form the reefs which the spongy reef corals construct. Small coral trees are generally available in rock and shell shops.

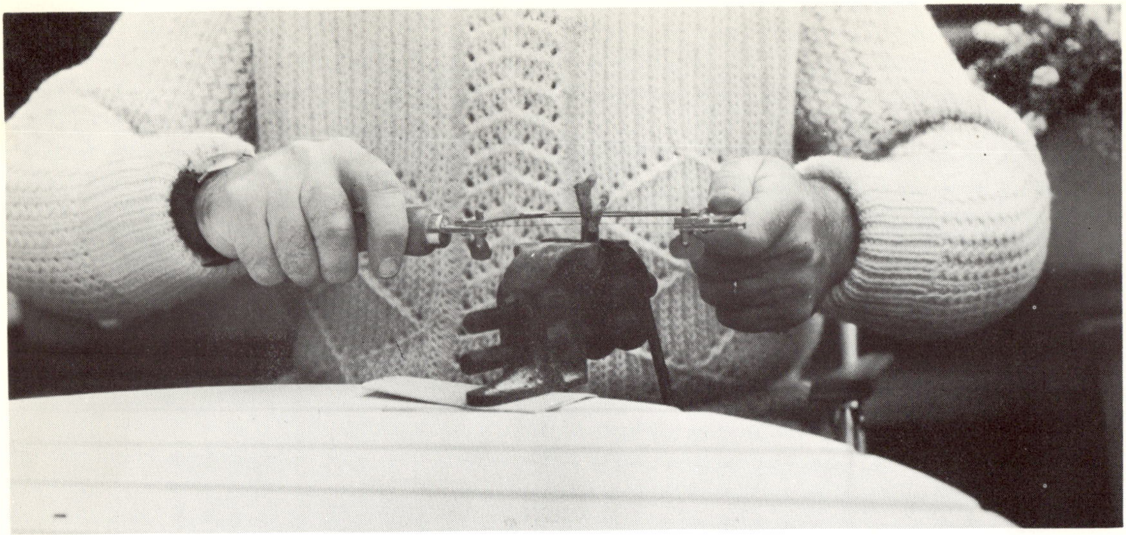

Illus. 40. Cutting through a coral branch held in a leather-lined vice, using a jeweler's saw.

Cuff Links, Earrings, and Rings

You can make a unique pair of cuff links from two "twigs" of a small coral bush. The coral has an easily crumbled outer layer called sarcosoma. Scrape this off, and, underneath, you will find the surface coveted with thin parallel lines. File or scrape these off with a wood-engraver's knife. When the surface is completely smooth, polish with fine sandpaper. If any lines still show, try scraping them off with a needle file.

Illus. 41. Small twigs of coral were filed and ground into shapes such as these and assembled in patterns on Italian goldsmith's work during the Renaissance.

Finish by polishing first with emery powder, then pumice powder, and finally tripoli powder. If you prefer, use kitchen cleanser, followed by powder used for cleaning silver plate. Place the stems in a mild solution of hydrogen peroxide and water to bring out their color. All you need do now is attach them to cuff-link findings with epoxy cement. You can also use such small stems for earrings.

To make a ring, you will need a ready-made finding. Shape the coral piece with a file until it is exactly the right size to fit the finding. Then flatten one side of it by rubbing on a piece of sandpaper. Polish and finish, and attach to the finding with epoxy cement.

Necklaces and Bracelets

For cuff links, earrings and rings, you did not have to drill the coral. However, for necklaces and bracelets or any pieces that you intend to string, you will have to drill. For drilling coral, use a jeweler's drill, sometimes called a "pump drill" or "Archimedean" drill.

Stick the coral piece to your bench with a dab of dop wax. Make a guide hole by twirling the point of a knife in the exact middle of the twig. Position the drill precisely over the hole and drill carefully, lubricating the drill with water periodically so that it does not get too hot.

If you wish to shape the coral into symmetrical beads, use twigs that have stem thicknesses equal to the widest part of your intended bead size. Drill holes as before and then slip the pieces of coral onto the bead holder described in making ivory beads (page 24). Shape carefully with a file, and then polish as before.

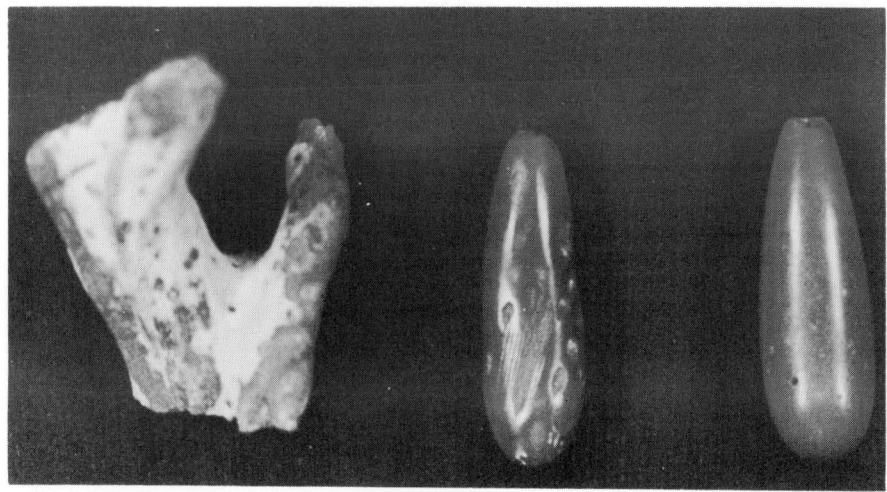

Illus. 42. Three stages in making a coral earring: First, saw the raw coral into a blank (left). Next, shape it roughly and partially polish it with a file (middle). Finally, polish it completely smooth with sandpaper, abrasives and polishing compounds (right). It is now ready to be mounted on a finding.

31

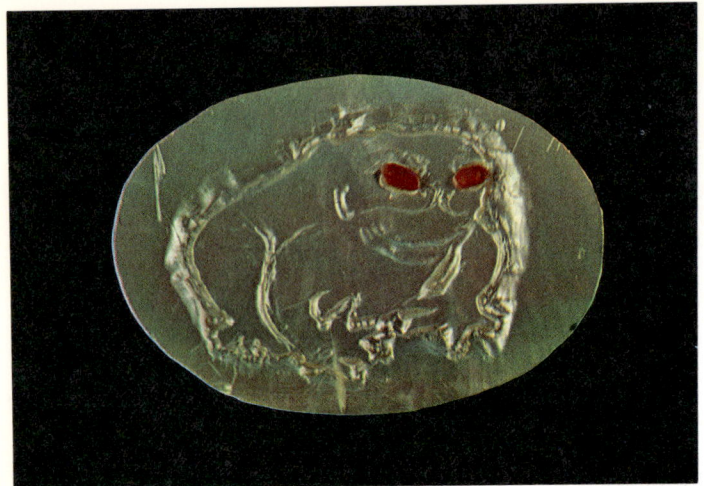

Illus. 43. A mother-of-pearl brooch with a carved design and coral eyes.

Illus. 44. This mother-of-pearl pendant has a cut-out tortoise shell design glued on it.

Illus. 45. A carved mother-of-pearl brooch. For polishing and finishing carved mother-of-pearl, see page 37.

Illus. 46. This mother-of-pearl pendant has a small carved mother-of-pearl star glued on.

33

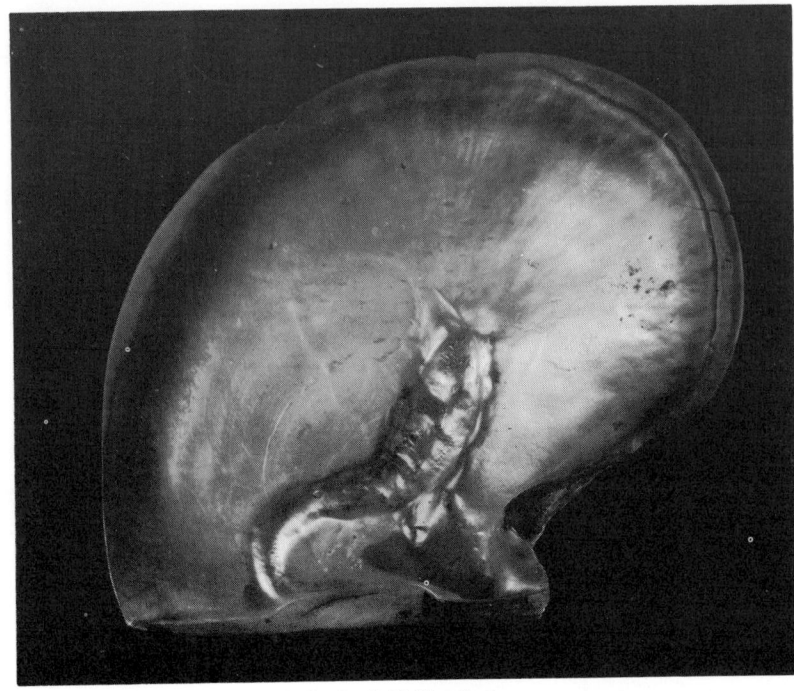

Illus. 47. Trapped inside the mollusc's shell, a small fish was completely covered with mother-of-pearl.

Illus. 48 (Below). Pearl shell jewelry of this type was made in Bethlehem (19th century ?) and is available to pilgrims to the Holy Land.

From "Pearls in Pictures," © 1966 by Sterling Publishing Co. Inc.

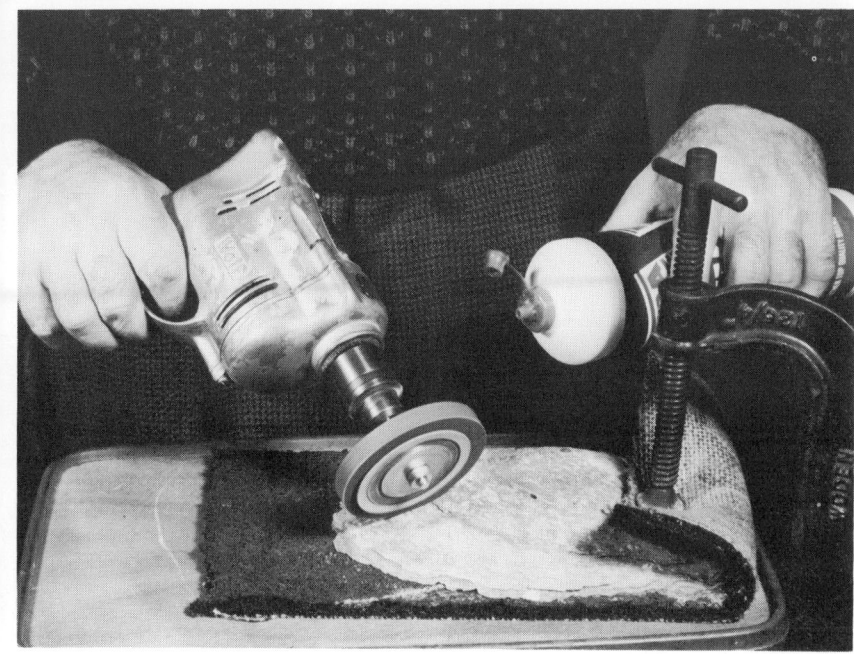

Illus. 49. As you grind away the hard outer crust, use an empty plastic soap bottle as a bellows to blow away the dust that accumulates on the shell.

Mother-of-Pearl

Mother-of-pearl is the iridescent substance that forms the lining of the shells of some fresh-water and salt-water molluscs. Like the pearl, it is a secretion of the mantle, and is found chiefly in the pearl oyster and mussel. Although you probably think of it as button material, it is excellent for all kinds of jewelry.

Shell shops carry the big pearl oyster from the Orient and South Pacific, which you will undoubtedly wish to tackle at some point. A shell warehouse will supply you with "scabby" pearl oyster shells which are worn, pitted, and have blemishes. However, you can usually cut them up in such a way to avoid using the blemished parts.

Begin by grinding off the hard, horny, brown layer covering the outside of the shell, using a grindstone held in an electric drill (Illus. 49). Then use a hacksaw to saw the shell into pieces. A coping saw is particularly useful for getting round corners, and if you have any fine cutting to do, such as round outlines, use a fret saw with a metal cutting blade.

You can make a lovely mother-of-pearl pendant very simply (Illus. 50). Place the shell on

35

Illus. 50. A mother-of-pearl pendant with carved tortoise shell. (See color Illus. 44).

Carving

Mother-of-pearl is fairly tough to carve, and you may prefer to use a power tool for the carving. (If so, use a rotary file fixed in a flexible drive worked by a power drill.)

Stick the piece of shell to be carved down on a flat surface with a dab of dop wax or beeswax. Draw the pattern on the surface of the shell with India ink and a mapping pen (Illus. 1). Shade the parts of the design which are to be hollow, and scoop them out with a rotary file. Then, cut in the fine lines and details of the carving with a graver.

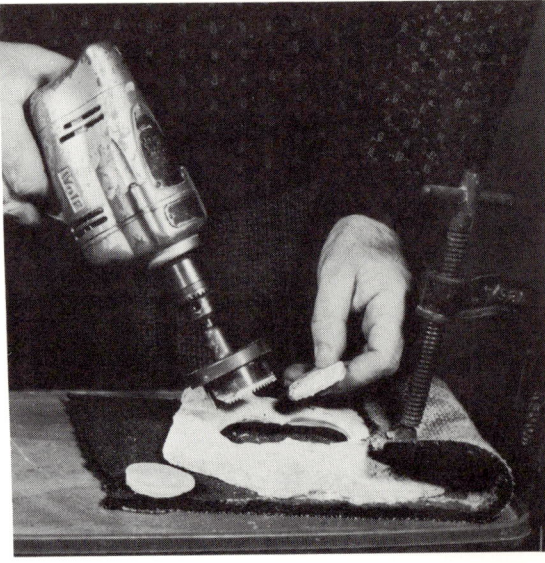

Illus. 51. Hold the mother-of-pearl shell down on a piece of carpet folded over and clamped as shown here. Use a hole-cutter held in an electric drill to cut your blanks.

a piece of old carpeting. Fold over the end of the carpeting and clamp down (Illus. 51). Use a hole-cutter held in an electric drill to make the blank. Once cut out, smooth the edges and both sides with a file and sandpaper.

You can also easily make mother-of-pearl jewelry consisting entirely of pierced work. First, outline your pattern on the shell. Then, drill all the holes which will admit the piercing-saw blade. Cut out the parts to be removed, and finish by cleaning out the holes cut with the saw with needle files. (See Illus. 52.)

36

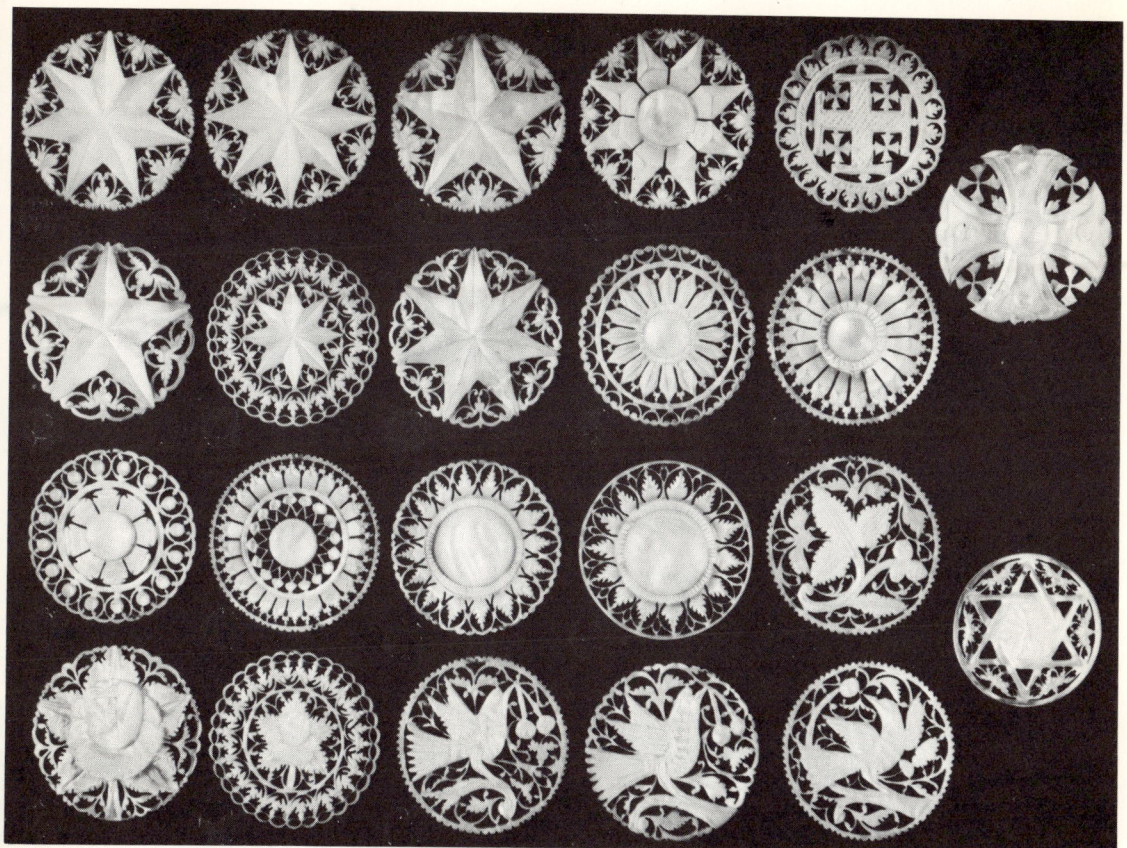

Illus. 52. These beautiful mother-of-pearl brooches, made by craftsmen in Bethlehem, have pierced designs that you can create yourself using your piercing-saw blade.

Use gouges and V-shaped cutting chisels to render all the finer points of the design.

Finish by brushing the carving with emery powder or powdered pumice stone, applied wet with a brush. Next, polish the piece with a mixture of water and tripoli powder, followed by putty powder. Give a final polish with a cloth dipped in a solution of copper sulphate dissolved in water. (Oxalic acid, in the mild solution applied to marble statuary, can also be used as a final polish.)

37

Illus. 53. This 19th century Chinese scratch carving was made for use as a counter while playing cards. Such scratch carvings make beautiful brooches or pendants.

Another means of ornamenting mother-of-pearl is by "scratch carving." Draw a design on the surface of the piece and engrave all the lines *lightly* with a veiner. You can leave the lines plain or fill with India ink, as suggested for ivory on page 26.

Cameos

Probably the most popular of all shell carvings is the cameo. Cameos can be made from any kind of shell with one or more layers of color in it. Some of these are: the black helmet (chocolate brown and white); the bull mouth (white and orange); the horned helmet (white and orange); the king helmet (white and brown); the tiger cowrie (white and dark brown); the panther cowrie (white and dark brown); the gold ringer (grey and black); the snake's-head cowrie (white and violet); the money cowrie (white and violet); and the poached egg (white and dark red).

The big shells such as the helmets mentioned above, provide the thickest cameo material with the greatest amount of relief, but they require a good deal of cutting up, so try your first cameo carving on the smaller, easier-to-handle cowries. In addition, the cowries are less expensive and have exciting colors. Draw your pattern with

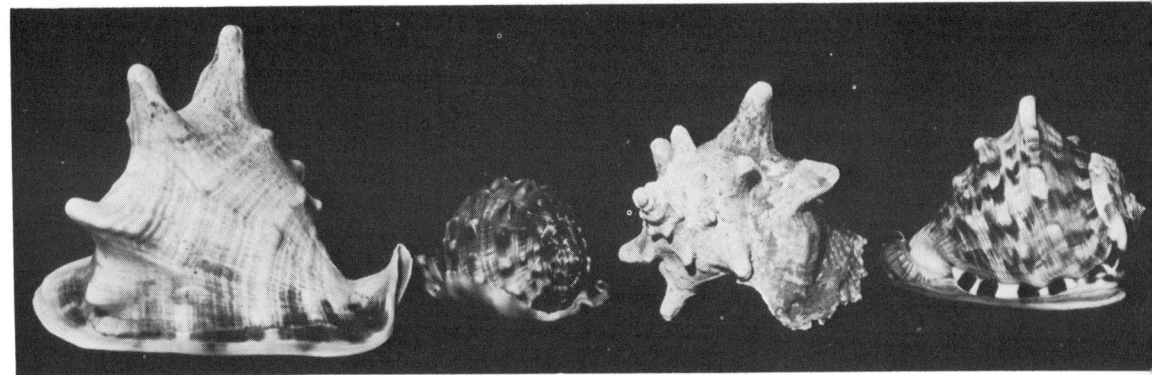

Illus. 54. These large shells are used by professional jewelry-makers to cut cameos. Although big shells such as these afford the thickest cameos, they require a good deal of cutting, so begin your cameo-making on smaller shells, such as the cowries.

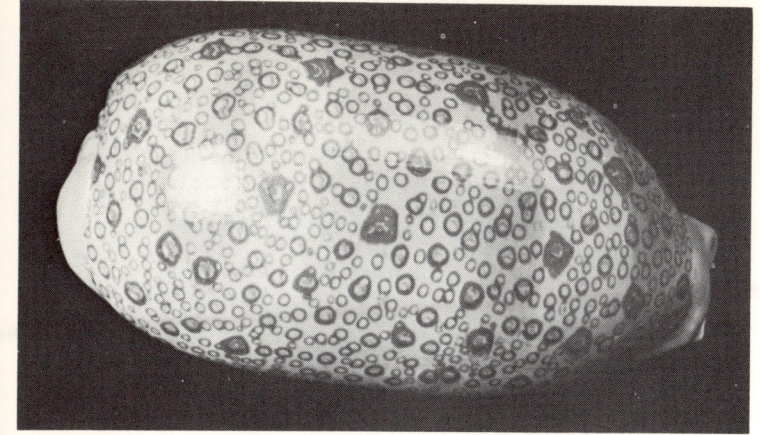

India ink on the surface of the shell, marking the parts of the carving you want to cut away. Then stick down the shell on the end of a circular wooden dowel with dop wax (Illus. 56). File the surface of the shell until you reach the next layer of color. Then block out the profile with strokes of the file. Cut away the outside of the profile with gravers. Polish the completed carving with powdered pumice stone, applied dry with a brush.

When you have succeeded in making satisfactory cameos with the cowries and decide to go on to the big shells, cut them up with a hacksaw into blanks the right size for each cameo. Grind the hard outer layer off with a grindstone and use gravers to cut away the design in the middle layer.

Because the best helmet shells are used by professional cameo carvers, you will find that many of the ones you buy have "fugitive" colors beneath the first layer. This is particularly true of the bull mouth. The black helmet and horned helmet are most likely to have a good color layering. Polish these cameos in the same way as you polish the cowrie cameos.

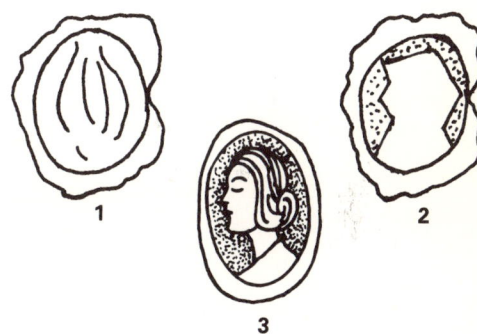

Illus. 56. Steps in making a cameo: (1) Stick the cowrie down on the end of wooden dowel with dop wax. (2) Cut the surface down with a file until you reach the next layer of color. Block out profile by strokes of the file. (3) Cut in detail with gravers and other cutting tools.

Wood

Wood jewelry has probably the most readily-available source of supply of any of the organic materials you have worked on thus far. Any old piece of wood furniture or other attractive scrap of wood has a potential in jewelry-making. If you want really exotic woods, shop around at a furniture-maker's or in a lumber yard. However, most woods can be found in a junk shop.

Beads

Ebony and mahogany can be made into attractive beads which you can file to shape on the bead holder shown in Illus. 24. Smooth and polish in the same manner as for polishing coconut (page 11).

You can make round beads very simply. Saw a piece of hard wood to a length that will accommodate the number of beads you require. Use a metal template the exact width of the bead to

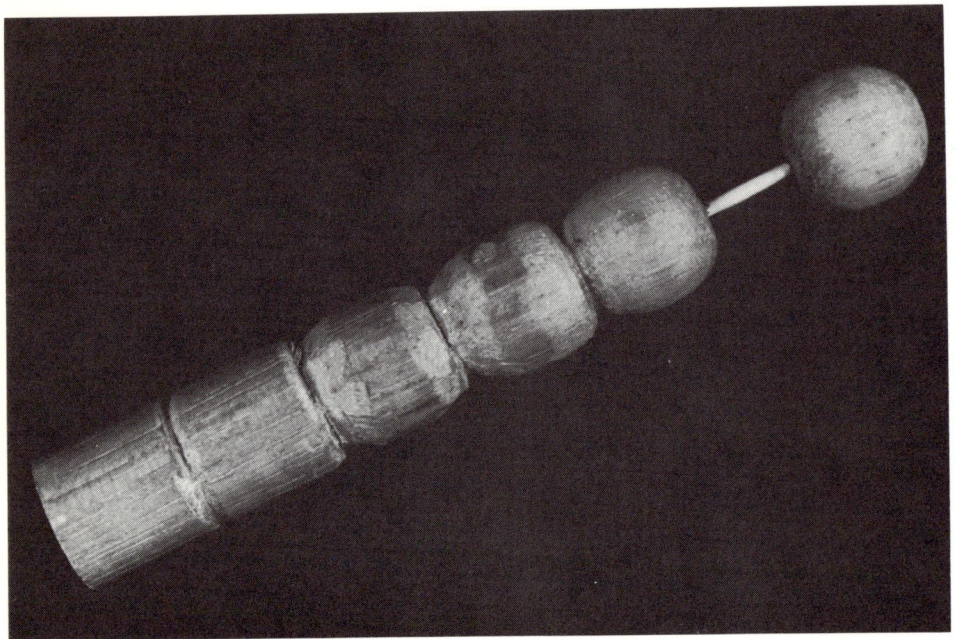

Illus. 57. Stages in making a wooden bead: First, outline the area on a round wooden dowel with a saw. Next, deepen the outline with a triangular file. Then whittle chips of wood away to produce a rough rounded shape. Rough out further with a file. Finish with sandpaper and emery boards, and saw off.

scribe lines on the wood (Illus. 57) with a sharp style (Illus. 1). Round off the sharp corners with a file (Illus. 57). Cut a groove with a triangular file along each of the scribe marks and then saw each bead off with a jeweler's saw. This will leave a clean cut and save on later smoothing.

Drill each bead through the exact middle and thread them all on a wire stretched between two screws on a board (Illus. 31). Rub them down all at once with fine sandpaper.

Pendants

The simplest and probably most effective wood pendant you can make is a piece of wood worked into one very large bead in the same way as above. Drill a large hole through the middle and slip on a looped leather thong. Tie a knot with the two ends just below the hole to prevent the pendant from slipping off.

You might want to make a pierced design. Use a piercing saw to cut out the unwanted parts of the pattern. Round and shape the pendant with a file before finishing with fine sandpaper.

Chip Carving

Chip carving is another method of ornamenting jewelry. It consists of carving regularly repeating geometrical patterns which are composed of tiny hollows made by gougework—three cuts of a knife—leaving an incised triangular recess (Illus. 59a). Chip carving can be found in many parts of the world, where primitive people applied it to war clubs, knife handles, and even on gypsy pan-pipes (Illus. 59b).

You can use a craft knife, a wood engraver's knife, small graver and gouger, triangular file, or any other tool which will enable you to turn sharp corners. It is easiest to execute in a fairly hard wood such as mahogany, walnut, holly, or ebony.

You must first draw a master design so that the finished product is meticulously symmetrical, with every element occupying an equal space. Use graph, or squared, paper to help you. Then transfer the design with great care to the surface of the wood. Go over the transferred design, and pencil in any part not clearly defined.

Never polish a finished chip-carved piece of

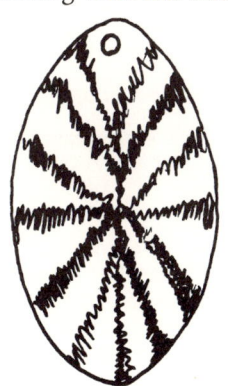

Illus. 58. A pokerwork pendant. Take a spoon-shaped piece of white softwood, whittle into shape, and char the design on with either an electric soldering iron, or nail held in an insulating handle, which you keep red hot by dipping it into a flame.

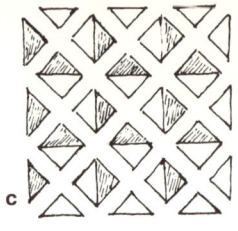

a   b c

Illus. 59. Chip carving: (a) gougework chip carving; (b) chip-carved patterns from a Bulgarian Gypsy panpipe; (c) simple chip-carved pattern.

jewelry. The only polish should be that created by the sharp edge of a tool.

Silver Inlays

The beautiful Bosnian wood and silver designs in Illus. 61 look incredibly intricate to the beginner. However, all of them are built up from just a few simple elements.

The first essential is to choose your wood well. Silver wire combines especially nicely with mahogany and walnut. White woods, such as holly, do not provide a good contrast with silver, but you might inlay them with gilt or copper wire or brass wire. Make a very simple drawing in pencil on a piece of paper the same size as the piece you are going to ornament. Trace it onto the surface of the wood after shaping and smoothing the wood. Next, engrave the design with a wood-engraver's graver, cutting in just deep enough to accommodate the wire.

Illus. 60. This is how the simplest form of the well known Tunbridge Ware jewelry is made, and you can do it easily. Cut sections from a triangular ivory rod. Then glue them to triangular sections of wood. Smooth and polish, and use as cuff links or earrings.

Cut the silver wire to the exact length of each line to be inlayed, place some wood cement in the grooves, and then press the wire in with the point of a bone folder.

This method is best if you are ornamenting a round surface. However, there is a quicker method you can use when the surface of the jewelry is fairly flat. Cut the piece from mahogany so that its surface is at right angles to the grain of the wood. Bend the wire, using round-nosed pliers, into the exact shape you want. Lightly smear the underside of the bent wire with wood cement, and lay it on the wood. Tap the wire lightly into the wood with a leather or rubber mallet.

If your design is elaborate, assemble the whole wire inlay and glue it down on a piece of paper the same size as the piece of jewelry. Be sure to use water-soluble glue for this purpose. When it has dried, smear a little wood cement on the wire and stick it down, wire-side on the bottom, on top of the wood. Proceed to tap it into the wood. When the wood cement has had a chance to set, wet the paper and remove it carefully.

Whichever method you use, once the wire is sunk into the wood, you must smooth it down with a fine file till it lies flat with the wood. Do this very, very carefully or you might raise the wire. Then smooth down both the wire and the wood with very fine sandpaper until the surface is smooth and nicely polished.

Jewelry that is in constant use, such as a ring, will not tarnish. However, a piece that is inlaid with silver wire that you do not use often will benefit by a coat of polyurethane varnish. First, clean the surface of the jewelry with a rag dipped in denatured alcohol. Then, brush on a coat of thinned varnish, using a sable brush. Rub down this first coat with fine sandpaper as soon as it is dry. Follow with other coats, allowing each to dry and sanding each one.

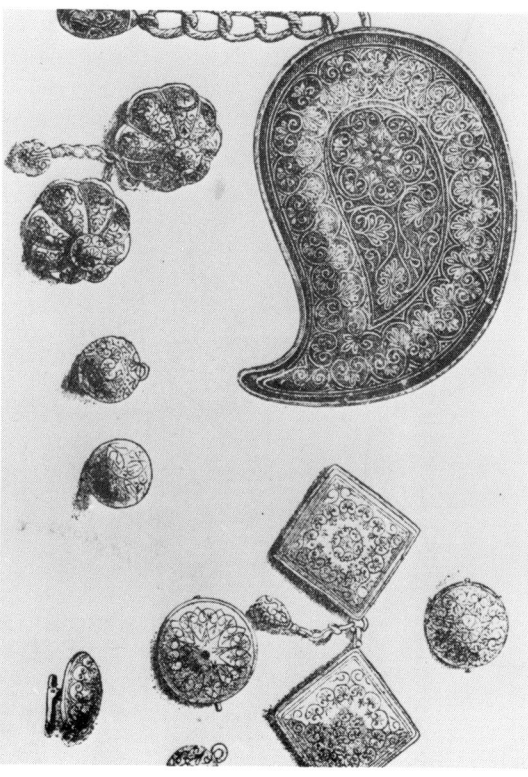

Illus. 61. Nineteenth-century Bosnian wood jewelry inlaid with silver looks intricate, but you need only learn a few basic elements to reproduce it.

Jet, Cannel Coal, and Lignite

Illus. 62. Whitby jet jewelry by Edward Hewland Pearson.

Illus. 63. A block of jet.

Jet is fossilized driftwood. Cannel coal and lignite are fossilized plant material. Jet is the least common of the three, but it is the easiest to carve. Lignite is a form of soft coal, present in such large quantities that a whole industry developed round it. The Aztecs used lignite in mosaics, and the American Pueblo Indians made beautiful jet jewelry inlaid with turquoise.

You can acquire jet from a rock or mineral supply house or hobby shop. Although more beads are made of jet than any other kind of jewelry, it is a very versatile material. You can carve it with a knife, or work it into fretted pieces with a fret saw.

Begin work on your selected piece by marking out the design with a white china marker or a mapping pen dipped in Chinese white. Saw it out with a piercing saw, lubricating the blade by wiping with a damp sponge periodically. Then

Illus. 64. Cameo head by Edward Hewland Pearson, and the knife which he used to carve jet.

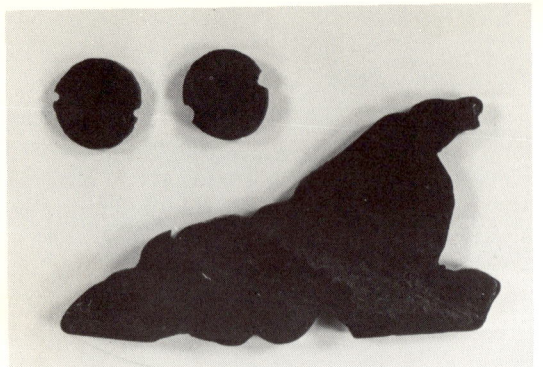

Illus. 65. (Left) Blanks for jet jewelry. The large piece shows the rough surface of the jet after being sawn with the jeweler's saw. The two earring blanks were cut from a circular section left in the middle of a ring. (Right) The large jet blank, carved and polished, and ready to be mounted as a brooch.

use files or rifflers (small sculpture rasps) to work it into shape. Smooth the piece with fine sandpaper.

For carving a design (Illus. 65), use a wood-engraver's knife. This is very similar to the traditional jet carver's knife shown in Illus. 64.

When you are satisfied with your carving, polish it by wetting a cloth with either almond oil or olive oil and rubbing the jet as hard as you can with it. Use jeweler's rouge for the next polish, rubbing it on with another cloth dipped in oil. You will see the jet turn from a brown color to a glossy black. When you can see your face in the polished surface, the polishing is complete.

Lignite and cannel coal are rather similar. Although lignite tends to crack, you can steep it in a strong solution of white shellac and denatured alcohol until it is hard enough to carve. Both cannel coal and lignite can be carved and polished in the same way as jet.

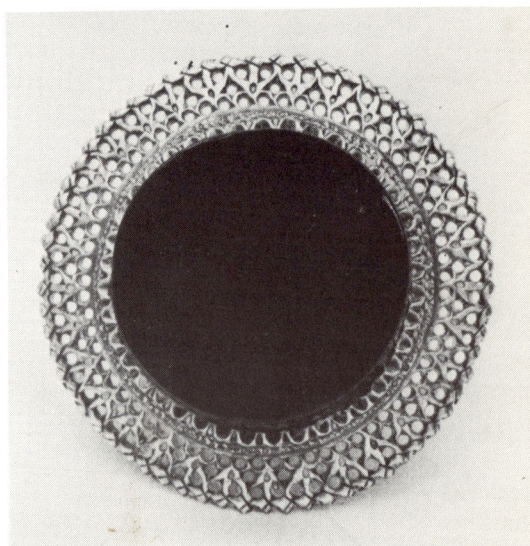

Illus. 67. A very large jet ring made by the author and mounted in a 19th-century Indian ring setting.

46

Suppliers of Organic Materials and Equipment

Allcraft Tool and Supply Company, Inc.
215 Park Avenue
Hicksville, New York 11801
Power and hand tools, jewelry findings, horn

Astro Minerals Ltd.
155 East 34th Street
New York, New York 10016
Ivory

Friedlein Natural Products
Kudu House
The Minories, E.C.3, London, England
Ivory and tortoise shell; ivory and tortoise shell offcuts; shells of all kinds, including mother-of-pearl

Fukushima Coral & Co. Ltd.
Kochi-shi
Kochi, Japan
Coral

Glamour International Traders (E.A.) Ltd.
P.O. Box 660
Mombasa, Kenya
Exotic nuts and seeds

Ikeda Coral Shop
Obiyamachi
Kochi
Japan
Coral

Indiacraft
59,63 Islington Park Street
London N11 QE, England
Exotic nuts and seeds

International Gem Corporation
15 Maiden Lane
New York, New York 10038
Bone, horn, ivory, commercial polishing powders for bone and horn

Donald Kostecki
6245 N. Fairfield
Chicago, Illinois 60659
Ivory: walrus teeth, whale teeth, hippopotamus teeth, elephant ivory, old ivory chunks, strips

Maendeleo ya Wanawake Organization
P.O. Box 4412
Nairobi, Kenya
Exotic nuts and seeds

Seashells Unlimited, Inc.
590 Third Avenue
New York, New York 10016
Shells

Index